PABLO ESCOBAR
Narcos King

The World's Most Infamous Gangster

Roger Harrington

Copyright © 2017.

All rights reserved. No part of this publication may be reproduced, distributed, or transmitted in any form or by any means, including photocopying, recording, or other electronic or mechanical methods, without the prior written permission of the publisher, except in the case of brief quotations embodied in critical reviews and certain other noncommercial uses permitted by copyright law.

This book is intended for informational and entertainment purposes only. The publisher limits all liability arising from this work to the fullest extent of the law.

Table of Contents

A Corpse On A Rooftop

Escobar's Columbia

Rise To Power

Politics

La Catedral

Search Bloc

The End

Aftermath

Voices

A Corpse On A Rooftop

The city of Medellin is the second-largest in the South American nation of Columbia. It is nestled in the Aburra Valley in the Andes ranges.

On December 2 1992 citizens of the district of Los Olivos heard gunshots from the rooftops. They saw two men running across the orange – tiled roofs, pursued by a group of armed and uniformed men.

A short gunfight ensued. Soon eight armed men, officers of the National Columbian Police, posed for photographs, brandishing weapons and smiling over the bloody corpse of a 44-year-old man.

That man was Pablo Emilia Escobar Gaviria, known in the annals of infamy simply as Pablo Escobar.

He had been the most powerful drug lord in Colombia and one of the most notorious in the world.

He was so pernicious that for a time he was number one on the hit list of the United States. He controlled the cocaine trade in the United States.

He used wealth and terror to dominate Columbian politics and destroy his enemies.

He openly flaunted his fantastic wealth, believing that he was untouchable.

But there he was, a bare-footed, bloody corpse, his executioners shouting 'Viva Columbia! Viva Columbia!'

So who was this man?

Pablo Escobar was born on November 1 1949 in the Columbian city of Rionegro.

His father, Abel de Jesus Dari Escobar was a peasant father of moderate means.

His mother was Hermilda Gaviria, a school teacher.

Pablo was the third of seven children.

His parents were poor and suffered hardship. Pablo had to work far to school and he had only one pair of shoes. When these wore out he walked barefoot.

He was humiliated by his teacher and sent back home. Hermilda had no money to buy shoes and so stole some.

Smitten by remorse she confessed to a priest and returned the shoes. She was allowed to buy a pair on credit.

Pablo comforted his mother, saying 'Don't worry, mom, wait until I grow up, I will give you everything.'

Pablo's father was away for long periods in the field. His mother not only had to look after seven children but hold down her job as a teacher.

The Gaviria children had to learn independence and resilience in their hard world.

There were light moments, however, such as when their mother would regale them with stories of their paternal grandfather Roberto, who was a whiskey smuggler.

In these stories the wily Roberto would always outwit the authorities with new and adventurous schemes.

During Pablo's childhood Columbia was in the throes of a civil war. From 1948 to 1958 the Columbian Conservative Party and the Columbian Liberal Party fought for control of the country.

About 25,000 armed combatants perished in the conflict, but the brunt of the savagery was born by the civilian population. Millions were forced to flee their homes and abandon their property. Up to 300,000 were killed.

This terrible conflict was called simply *La Violencia*. Bloodletting and torture became so familiar to the people that names for them entered the Columbian lexicon.

Pica para tamal was the slow cutting away of flesh from someone until they died.

Bochachiquiar involved inflicting tiny punctures, causing the victim to slowly bleed to death.

Then there was the *Corbata Columbiana* or Columbian neck-tie, where the victim's tongue would be pulled through a horizontal slash in the victim's neck.

Crucifixions were commonplace. People were thrown from planes in mid-flight. Schoolgirls as young as eight were raped. Infants were torn from their mothers' wombs and replaced by roosters.

Children were bayonetted. Ears were cut off. The barbarities seemed endless.

A child growing up in these times might very well be accustomed to violence as a way of life.

La Violencia was precipitated by the assassination of Jorge Gatan, the leader of the Liberal Party and a presidential candidate in 1948.

It was widely believed that the CIA was responsible for the killing. The United States did indeed have an interest in keeping the anti-Communist Conservative Party in power.

The death of a populist leader who had pledged to help the poor, ostensibly at the hands of the US must have influenced the boy Escobar's anti-US views later on.

From an early age Pablo had drive and ambition. He wanted to rise above his condition. He wanted to become President of Columbia by the age of 30. He also wanted to become a millionaire by the age of 22.

It seems however that from an early age he chose a criminal path toward success.

As a child he was engaged in street crime.

As a teenager he stole gravestones and sanded them down for resale. He also sold counterfeit high school diplomas and stole cars.

There was a side to Escobar that was socially conscious. At the tender age of 13 he was elected President of his school's Council for Student Wellness. This group advocated for the poor.

He rebelled against authority. He began to skip school. When his mother discovered that he had not attended school in 2 years she sent him back.

Escobar protested. He preferred the education the Medellin gangs could give him. 'Mother, I keep on telling you, I want to be big, I want to be big,' he said. 'And I will be… I'm poor but I will never die poor, I promise.'

Inevitably he was expelled and he settled into lie as a street criminal.

As a youth he vowed to rise above his own poverty and labor against poverty. Later in life he would be known to many of the poor in Columbia as their nation's Robin Hood.

Escobar did go to the Universidad Autónoma Latinoamericana in Medellin. This seemed strange given his disillusionment with traditional education. Perhaps he believed a future President of Columbia would need a degree. Whatever the motivation, he left without obtaining it.

By the age of 20 Escobar was already a legend in Medellin. His cool, dead-pan style of robbing banks without even threatening the bank teller with the rifle he carried attracted men to him.

Soon he had his own gang. One of these first gang members said 'He was like a God, a man with a very powerful aura. When I met him for the first time it was the most important day of my life.'

From now on, he would never again dirty his own hands. Instead he had only to command something and it would be done.

Escobar's Columbia

Columbia has a long history of violence and political instability.

In 1819, after a period of war, the Spanish Viceroyalty of New Granada became an independent republic, Granada.

Soon the country was divided between Conservatives and Liberals. Both parties struggled for power and both parties produced presidents for Columbia. Violent conflict between them was sporadic.

A terrible civil war erupted between the two in 1899. The Thousand Days War, which lasted 1,130 days, ended the lives of 120,000 Columbians. This was from a population of little more than 4,200 000.

Child soldiers featured in this conflict, as in the most of the nineteenth-century conflicts in Columbia.

We have already seen the origins of *La Violencia*. It ended in 1958 when Conservatives and Liberals agreed to share government. This 'National Front' government would have alternating Liberal and Conservative Presidents, each running for four-year terms for 16 years.

This arrangement did not satisfy all however.

Disaffected Liberal and Communist peasant communities formed armed bands which fought National Front forces.

These units coalesced into the Revolutionary Armed Forces of Columbia, or FARC.

There were also Far Right paramilitary groups.

Both sides financed themselves by kidnapping and drug trafficking.

The United States government was keenly interested in Columbian politics. Columbia is in the north-west of South America and borders the Panama Isthmus, the narrow stretch of land that joins South America to North America.

In fact the small nation of Panama had been part of Columbia until it declared independence, with US support, in 1903. Panama granted permission to the United States to build the Panama Canal and also granted the US sovereign rights over the canal.

The Panama Canal is an important conduit of trade for the United States and its integrity is vital to its interests.

The regime in Columbia is therefore of great interest to the United States.

During the Cold War it sought to protect the canal from Communist influence and protect US business interests in Columbia, and so supported Conservative forces in Columbia.

This then was the Columbia in which hundreds of thousands of poor youths of Escobar's generation grew up in – crippled by poverty, torn by factions and rendered lawless by armed thugs, drug lords and terrorists.

It was a major battleground of the Cold War and became the plaything of international capitalism and communism.

Many of these youths, Escobar included, experienced a regime bathed in blood and mired in corruption since before they were born. It could offer them no hope.

So they turned to crime.

Rise To Power

Drug trafficking was rife in Escobar's Colombia. As we have mentioned, it was a major source of financing for the FARQ and other paramilitary groups, both of the Left and the Right.

In 1982 the production of cocaine in Colombia surpassed that of coffee (Colombia is the fourth largest producer of coffee in the world).

In general these warlords were not directly involved in the production and distribution of cocaine and opiates. Rather they protected and encouraged operations in return for a cut in the profits.

Drug cartels supplied (and continue to supply) large quantities of product into the

United States, generating fantastic incomes for ruthless drug lords.

For a man like Escobar, dreaming of political power in Columbia, the road to power was paved in cocaine. Whoever controlled the paramilitary organizations controlled the country. Anyone who could dominate the drug trade could dominate them.

Would-be President Escobar therefore had to first reign over the drug lords.

Escobar began his operation in 1975 by buying raw cocaine in Peru and refining it in Medellin. Then it would be smuggled into the United States, where demand for cocaine was high.

Soon Escobar was making $500,000 per trip.

His first air fleet consisted of 9 planes and 6 helicopters.

In 1976 Escobar and a few of his men were arrested on a return trip from Equador, in possession of 39 pounds (18 kilograms) of raw cocaine.

The mugshot taken of him at the time shows a smiling, confident man who appears in total control of his situation.

He attempted to bribe the judges who would decide his case. This failed.

Then his lawyers wrangled for the charges to be dropped. This too failed.

Finally Escobar resolved on a solution that was as simple as it was final. He ordered the murder of the two arresting officers.

Without their testimony the case had to be dropped.

Escobar himself acknowledges this as the point where he realized he could use murder as a tool to what he wanted. He used this tool regularly.

In fact he ruthlessly ordered the murder of hundreds, if not thousands of people in a reign of terror designed to protect and advance his operations.

Anyone who got in his way was removed.

'…I am God,' he said. 'If I say a man dies, he dies the same day.'

More than 3000 died by his command.

He usually killed his victims in one of two ways – *'plata o plomo'*. *Plata* was accepting a bribe. *Plomo* was a bullet.

Escobar's notable victims included Fabio Restrepo, a Medellin trafficker whose demise in 1975 meant that Escobar controlled all crime in Medellin.

Escobar's hitman was one John Jairo Velasquez, also known as Popeye.

Velasquez was born in the province of Antioquia. He joined the army, navy and police force briefly before falling into the Medellin crime scene.

He soon came to Escobar's attention. He chose him as his hitman and brought him into his inner circle.

Velasquez's loyalty to Escobar was total. On one occasion Escobar discovered that Velasquez's girlfriend was an informant.

'You or her,' Escobar told him. 'Do not hesitate a single second.'

Velasquez killed her.

Velasquez was arrested on charges of terrorism, drug trafficking and murder. In 1992 he was imprisoned.

He was released in 2014 He now speaks on a YouTube channel on topics related to crime and politics.

He calls himself '*Arrepentido*' (repentant), though many criticize him for capitalizing on his notoriety.

The demand for cocaine in the United States increased and Escobar stepped up his operation.

He founded his own drug cartel in Medellin, in partnership with a number of other drug lords.

The key members of the Cartel, beside Escobar, were Carlos Lehder, Jose Gonzalo Rodriguez, George Jung and the three Ochoa brothers Jorge, Juan David and Fabio.

Escobar's partnership with Lehder was instrumental in increasing supply to the United States.

Lehder started his criminal career supplying stolen vehicles for his family's used car business. From there he moved into the cocaine trade.

He used Norman's Cay, a small island in the Bahamas, as a shipment base.

The island rapidly became a haven for drug traffickers and a place where they could party.

One visitor to the island described being picked up at the airfield by naked women. 'It was a Sodom and Gomorrah,' he said.

The government of the Bahamas turned a blind eye to Norman's Cay until pressure from the US forced it to confiscate the property in 1987.

The Medellin Cartel organized the shipment of about 80 tons of cocaine to the United States every month.

His methods of smuggling cocaine were ingenious.

One such method involved soaking jeans in liquid cocaine. When they arrived in the United States the dried jeans would be soaked again so that the cocaine could be extracted from the liquid by evaporation.

He was making $420,000,000 a week and supplied about 80% of the US cocaine demand.

Escobar lived in style. He purchased an estate in called Hacienda Napoles in the region of Antioquia, of which Medellin was the capital.

Hacienda Napoles covered 20 square kilometers. There is an old colonial house on the estate, as well as a private zoo full of exotic animals such as elephants, antelope, giraffes, hippopotamuses and ostriches.

The ranch also had a collection of antique cars and bicycles, a kart-racing track, a private airport and a bullring.

In addition there were gigantic statues of dinosaurs constructed for Escobar's son, Juan Pablo.

At the entrance of the hacienda there is simple arch. On top of the arch is a small airplane.

This plane was one of Escobar's first. It was destroyed in a landing accident. The pilot, a friend of Escobar's, died.

Escobar reconstructed the plane and place it at the entrance of the hacienda both as a memorial of his friend and of his beginnings.

Nowadays Hacienda Napoles is operated as a theme park by the Colombian government.

Staff are deterred from speaking about its criminal past.

An Escobar legacy still survives in the hippopotamuses of his zoo. After his death the creatures went feral, living in the nearby waterways and forming a population which may be as large as 30.

In addition, 40 hippos still live on the estate.

The feral hippos terrorize the local population

And fishermen have called for culls.

In 1976 Escobar married Maria Victoria Henao Vellejo. The two had met in 1974. Escobar was 24. Vellejo was only 13.

Her family disapproved of the relationship but they started dating.

The real nature of their relationship has been a matter of speculation, though Maria stood by Escobar to the end, despite his many mistresses.

Perhaps she loved the life of luxury more than she loved him.

The couple had two children.

The first, Juan Pablo, was born in 1977. Father and son were close, though the peaceful Juan Pablo despised what his father did. He shunned and continues to shun any attempt to glorify his father's career.

After his father's death he went into exile with his mother and sister to Argentina, under the name Juan Sebastian.

He is now reaching out to the families of his father's victims to ask forgiveness on Escobar's behalf.

Escobar' daughter was born in 1984. Her name is Manuela.

Escobar doted on Manuela. He forced one of his mistresses to have an abortion because he had promised Manuela that she would be his last beloved child.

Manuela changed her name to Juana Manuela Marroquin Santos when she accompanied her mother and brother to Argentina. Unsurprisingly, she shuns attention and little is known of her.

Escobar knew that the arm of the United States was long. It had its agents in Colombia. It had influence with the Colombian Government and especially Conservative governments.

The United States had another reason for wanting to remove Escobar other than stopping his drug operations.

Escobar was anti-American, echoing the sentiments of many Colombians. If he had any genuine political affiliations they were with the Left. At least, that was the association that best opened doors for him.

The warlords of Colombia were financed by drugs. Whoever controlled the drug supply controlled the warlords, and whoever controlled the warlords controlled Colombia.

Therefore, in order to secure a friendly anti-communist regime in Colombia the United States had to eliminate Escobar.

Elected in 1982, President Belisario Betancur, a Conservative, initiated democratic reforms designed to alleviate the condition of the poor and reintegrate the military movements into Colombian society.

To this end he began negotiations with several guerrilla groups.

He was preparing to deal with the drug lords. He wanted to pass legislation that would allow the extradition of drug lords to the United States.

Escobar and the other drug lords were worried.

In August 1983 Betuncar appointed Rodrigo Lara as Minister of Justice.

Though a Liberal Rodrigo was picked by Betuncar for his tough stance against the cartels. In particular he targeted Escobar and the Medellin Cartel.

He denounced Escobar in the Colombian Congress, citing his involvement in the deadly drug trade. He also denounced him for interfering with politics and the media.

Escobar orchestrated a plot with politicians, drug traffickers and journalists to discredit Lara by creating evidence of his own supposed connection to drug traffickers.

The plot failed. Betuncar refused to accept that Lara was involved in organized crime. The concocted evidence, a check supposedly from a drug trafficker and a telephone call, were soon discredited.

With Betuncar's backing Lara then went after Escobar. He was expelled from Congress and his US visa was canceled.

The cancellation of his visa effectively made it difficult for Escobar to flee the country.

Lara revived charges against Escobar that had long remained dormant, and ordered the seizure of planes and property used for the distribution of cocaine.

Escobar retaliated with typical brutality.

On August 30 1984 Lara was driving down 127th Street in Bogota (now renamed in his honor).

An Escobar gunman, Ivan Dario Guisado, riding in a motorcycle, drew up beside the car and opened fire with a machine gun.

Lara's police escort returned fire, killing Darion and wounding the driver.

The wounded man, Byron Velasquez Arena, later confessed to being offered $20,800 to participate in the assassination.

Lara was taken to a nearby clinic but died shortly after being admitted.

Lara's death shielded Escobar from the government for a time but the Minister of Justice had destroyed his political status.

Moreover, it inflamed Betuncar against Escobar. Escobar's rivals could now also ride on the government's anger in their efforts to destroy him.

Escobar realized this immediately. The day after Lara's murder he telephoned his wife and sister.

His sister Luz Maria recounted 'When Lara Bonilla was murdered, we received a call from Pablo, and he said we had to leave our apartments in five minutes. So I packed my bags, my children's blankets and we began running, and this lasted for how many years. After Mr. Lara Bonilla's death, we had to run for ten years.'

Pablo himself fled to Panama with his family, where they was protected by General Manuel Noriega, President of Panama and himself a notorious drug lord ironically enjoying the support of the United States.

They escaped in a helicopter flying low so as to avoid radio.

It is perhaps evidence of the danger Escobar felt he was in that he sought the help of a man he did not trust. All the time he stayed in Panama he feared that Noriega might hand him over to the US.

What exactly Noriega had to gain by protecting Escobar is not clear, though we may safely assume that a great deal of money changed hands.

While he was staying with Noriega the President received Alfonso Lopez, a former President of Colombia and Betuncar's Liberal rival for the presidency in the 1982 campaign.

His presence lead to speculation that Escobar was using Lopez as an intermediary to offer to pay the national debt of Colombia in exchange for safe passage back to Colombia.

In fact all cartels were offering Betuncar that deal and they agreed that Escobar should be their spokesman. They wanted favors from the government and in particular freedom from extradition to the United States.

They also wanted amnesty for their crimes and they wanted to be left in possession of their fortunes.

Betuncar sent his attorney general to Panama but he ultimately refused. The price was too high.

Escobar continued to run the Medellin Cartel from Panama.

He and Noriega did not get on. Noriega stole an airplane and $3000 000 from him.

Escobar felt uneasy in Panama and with good reason. Panama was under the unrelenting gaze of the United States.

President Ronald Reagan's Administration was supporting Noriega in his fight against the Sandinistas, the socialist organization that ruled Nicaragua.

The US was financing an alliance against the Sandinistas known as the Contras.

US intelligence presence in the region was therefore intense. If Noriega could demonstrate a link between Escobar's operations and the Sandinista it might become useful for him to hand Escobar over.

In 1984 the US could not identify Escobar in Panama but it was surely just a matter of time.

Noriega fabricated a plot in which Escobar's men attempted to assassinate him and Noriega seized several drug labs.

Escobar fled to Nicaragua but he was flying from the frying pan into the fire.

Escobar was now associated with the Sandinistas and thus liable to be identified and seized by US intelligence.

While loading a shipment of cocaine on a plane Escobar and the drug lord Rodriguez Gacha were identified.

An informant, Barry Seal, had planted a camera on the nose of the plane.

The Reagan administration was delighted not so much by the identification of Escobar but by the establishment of a link between the Sandinistas and the Colombian drug traffickers. These would make it easier to secure funding from Congress for the Contras.

An indictment of Escobar was issued from Miami.

Escobar responded in typical form, assassinating Seal, who was living in Baton Rouge without witness protection.

He also exploded a car bomb in front of the residence of the US Ambassador in Bogota. The ambassador left the country.

Escobar needed to get back to Colombia and quickly.

He founded a pressure group in Colombia, named *Los Extraditabiles*, which opposed the extradition of Colombian citizens to the United States.

In November 1986 he wrote an extraordinary open letter to the Colombian people promising to end the violence in return for freedom from extradition.

In the letter he said 'we prefer a grave in Colombia over a prison cell in the United States.'

So Escobar and his family returned to Colombia. Escobar began waging war against Betuncar's government and its supporters.

He tried his usual tactic of bribery first to attempt to impede legislation that would allow the extradition of the drug lords.

When that failed he resorted to murder.

He murdered a Supreme Court judge. He murdered the editor of *El Espectador*, a major newspaper that supported the government.

The horrific murders continued. In parts of Medellin the slaughter was so great that signs were posted reading 'forbidden to dump bodies here.'

The horror achieved its aims and the extradition treaty with the United States was dropped.

Though the legislature had caved in Betuncar had not. He revived the possibility of an extradition treaty with the United States, referring the matter to the Supreme Court for study.

On November 6 1985 35 guerrillas of the Marxist M-19 movement attacked the Palace of Justice, the home of the Supreme Court of Colombia.

The assailants took 300 hostages, which included 43 judges and the Chief Justice.

Government forces rescued 200 of those hostages, but the siege lasted another day.

On November 7 the guerrillas sent a message inviting dialogue, but the decision had already been made to take back the Court by force.

By the end of the day the Court was back in government hands. More than 100 people died – hostages, government soldiers and guerrillas, including the guerrilla commander, Andres Almarales.

Among the dead were 12 magistrates.

What actually happened during the siege is still not entirely known. Recent investigations suggest that government forces may have killed some of the hostages themselves.

The siege was a tragedy for the dead and their families, a disaster for both the government and M-19, but a triumph for Pablo Escobar and the other drug lords.

All records in the court relating the *Los extraditabiles* – those drug lords under consideration for extradition to the United States- had been destroyed. Pablo Escobar's file in particular disappeared forever.

This destruction of the files was intensely embarrassing to Betuncar's government, which attributed the losses to government gunfire.

However it was widely known that Escobar himself had paid M-19 to assault the Supreme Court building and destroy the files relating to himself.

Escobar's own son confirmed that the attack was paid for by his father.

The siege had profound effects on the Betuncar's agenda. It sank his prospects of achieving peace with the warlords and effectively crippled the judicial system for a time.

Another serious threat to Escobar's interests came from the journalist and politician Luis Carlos Galan.

Galan was a senator and had served as Minister of Education in the ministry of President Misael Borrero from 1970 to 1972.

He had campaigned against Belisario Betancur in 1982 and nominated for the presidency again in 1987.

Galan was determined to put an end to the power of the drug cartels and of the Medellin Cartel in particular.

Galan and Escobar were associates of sorts. Both had been members of the New Liberalism movement, a dissident branch of the Liberal Party. Galan returned to the Liberals after New Liberalism's failure to gain the presidency in 1982.

Galan was charismatic, well-liked and powerful. He was a serious threat to both the Conservatives and the drug cartels.

Indeed he was not only a threat to these but to his own party as well. The Liberal Party had long been corrupted by drug money. If the cartels fell, then so would many of the leaders and powerbrokers in the Party.

Alberto Santofimio was one of those leaders. He had once served as Minister of Justice, which was ironic given what he did.

When it seemed that Galan could achieve the presidency easily Santofimio approached Escobar and asked him to assassinate Galan.

Escobar was probably planning to murder Galan anyway. In any case he was keen to oblige. He was furious with him for the way he had sidelined him in the New Liberal Movement, essentially barring him from a chance at the presidency.

At first Galan received death threats and threats to his children. Then came a first assassination attempt.

Escobar's hitman tried to kill him with a rocket-propelled grenade while he was visiting Medellin on August 4 1989.

The lack of subtlety and finesse in using such a weapon for an assassination was evidence of the fearlessness and audacity of the powers that wanted Galan dead.

After this attempt Galan's aides restricted his travels, but he would not be cowed. He did however accept advice not to go to the town of Soacha on August 18 1989. He was to attend an important football match there and address the crowd, which was expected to be large.

However, in one of those quirks of fate he changed his mind.

As Galan walked onto the platform to give a speech before 10,000 people, a shot rang out and Galan fell and died.

But if Escobar, Santofimio and their confederates believed they had removed the threat to their power they had grossly miscalculated.

The assassination did not cow the Colombian people. Instead it outraged them. Their fury is still evident today.

Hundreds of thousands of Colombians had invested all their hopes in this one man – the alleviation of their poverty, the end of the violence, the end of corruption, the reign of justice. Escobar had stolen something precious from them – hope.

The then President of Colombia, Virgilio Barco told the Colombian people 'Colombia is at war. We are at war with the drug traffickers and terrorists. We shall not rest until this war has been won.'

Barco immediately reinstated the US extradition treaty.

The Liberal Party swiftly nominated Galan's close associate and political ally Cesar Gaviria for the presidency.

Escobar stepped up his reign of terror. Thousands of Colombians were killed in car bombings. The bombs were placed in banks, offices, motels – everywhere.

The aim of the terror was to make the people feel unsafe. They would realize the impotence of the government to protect them and so force it to make peace with the cartels.

Escobar attempted to kill Gaviria as well. Gaviria booked a flight, Avianca 203, which was scheduled to fly from the capital, Bogota, to Cali in southwest Colombia.

The plane was destroyed by a bomb, killing all on board, while it was flying over Soacha on November 27 1989. Passengers and crew numbered 101.

The place over which it was destroyed was surely a reference to the assassination of Galan and a warning to any politician who would dare to take Escobar on.

But Gaviria was not on the plane. He had been warned by security not to board it.

On August 7 1990 Gaviria took the Oath of Office as President of Colombia.

Gaviria vowed not to bend to the power of the cartels. But still the terror continued and the government seemed powerless to stop it.

Gaviria would not bend. Neither would Escobar. It seemed as if the slaughter would continue

But then Escobar offered the government a deal.

La Catedral

Gaviria was not entirely powerless in the fight against the cartels. The savagery of Escobar's attacks was in fact testimony to Gaviria's successes.

Gaviria's attempts to extradite Escobar and other drug lords seemed close to bearing fruit. He was in close cooperation with US agencies.

He began offering immunity from extradition and reduced gaol time to traffickers who gave themselves up.

The strategy met with significant success. In the first few months of 1991 10 traffickers did so.

Three members of the Medellin Cartel surrendered themselves: Fabio and Jorge Luis, and David Ochoa.

This was a terrific coup for the government and a serious threat for Escobar. It now had intimate information about the Cartel and its operations.

The informants would surely be as helpful as they could, for they would be anxious for Escobar to be arrested or killed. Who knew if he could kill them in prison?

Rival cartels also saw Escobar as vulnerable and would undoubtedly take advantage.

In May 1991 an 82-year-old Catholic priest, Rafael Garcia Herreros approached the police with a surprising announcement.

Garcia, a well-known cleric who hosted a popular religious radio show, said that he had knelt down in prayer with Pablo Escobar.

'He is tired of hiding and he believes that Colombia can judge him with wisdom and justice,' he said. He would surrender himself to authorities in return for a guarantee of his safety.

As proof of his good intentions, Escobar released two kidnapped journalists.

The truth was that his enemies on every side were closing in. The Cali Cartel were his rivals, and increasingly more than rivals.

Though Medellin and Cali had cooperated in the past the latter was taking advantage of Escobar's weakness.

Escobar's minions were surrendering to the government or to rival cartels and his daughter had been recently injured in a bomb blast.

The government considered the offer seriously. The press was euphoric, decorating headlines with doves bearing olive branches.

But Escobar had conditions beyond protection for cartel death squads.

He told the government that the prison was to be designed and built to his own specifications. It was to be guarded by men of his own choosing. And of course he was not to be extradited to the United States where he was wanted on eight charges.

Gaviria agreed. The 'prison' was called *La Catedral*. It was less of a prison than a pleasure palace. It featured a football pitch, basketball court, discotheque and bar, as well as the usual luxuries Escobar was accustomed to – jacuzzis, a rotating bed and billiard tables.

Among the extravagances there was a telescope pointed at nearby Medellin, so Escobar could see his daughter while he spoke to her on the telephone.

Escobar received visitors in this prison and there were frequent parties. Prostitutes were brought in and alcohol flowed freely.

The purpose of the prison, as far as Escobar was concerned, was not to keep him in but to keep his enemies out. The government was prepared to accept this arrangement if it meant taking Escobar out of the drug trade.

His prison received its name because of its grandeur and opulence.

This terrible place has now assumed a quiet and peaceful purpose. It is a Benedictine monastery.

The word cathedral is derived from the Latin word *cathedra,* which was a bishop's seat of authority.

La Catedral became Escobar's new seat of power. He continued his operations and for Escobar this was ideal. He still enjoyed the freedom to operate as before and now he enjoyed government protection.

News of Escobar's activities leaked to the press. When Escobar tortured and killed four of his underlings over money in the grounds of his prison the government felt compelled to act.

Two officials went to *La Catedral* as if they were attending the court of a prince. They were the Deputy Minister of Justice and the chief of the prison system.

They both came unarmed and told Escobar that he was to be temporarily transferred from *La Catedral to* a conventional trial for his own security.

Escobar was of course not fooled. He already knew of the plan before the officials arrived. Escobar and his lieutenants debated whether to kill them while his hitman Velasquez waved a submachine gun at the officials.

News of the officials' detention swiftly reached Bogota. Colombian soldiers arrived to capture Escobar and rescue the government officials.

On July 22 1992 the soldiers attacked. Escobar's hostages were rescued, but Escobar himself escaped with most of his men.

Escobar had spent only 13 months of his 5 year 'prison' term. He disappeared into the forested mountains behind *La Catedral*.

It was suspected that a compliant guard force had allowed Escobar to escape. After all, he had chosen the guards himself and possibly had been bribed.

Escobar was free, though hunted by enemies on every side. The government was under intense to capture him. But they needed help.

They turned to the United States.

Search Bloc

The United States Joint Special Operations Command was created in 1980 to plan and execute security operations.

They have been employed in Afghanistan, Iraq, Pakistan, Libya, other areas. The organization has been credited with the killing of Osama Bin Laden in Pakistan in 2011.

The USJSO was assigned to train and advise a Colombian task force called Search Bloc.

Search Bloc had been created in 1989 by Gaviria with the express task of hunting down Pablo Escobar.

Members of Search Bloc were rigorously selected. One of their vital qualities had to be integrity.

They had to be impervious to corruption and fearless in the face of death.

Their commander was Colonel Hugo Martinez.

Martinez made an intense study of Escobar. He knew him intimately, even more than many of his close associates did.

He knew his habits, when he slept, how long he slept, what he would be doing at a given part of the day and what he liked to eat.

He knew Escobar preferred 14 or 15-year-old girls. He knew that he wore white Nikes. He knew the pet name he gave to his wife (Tata).

Martinez was apparently the only police officer who wanted to head Search Bloc. It was, after all, the most dangerous assignment in Colombia. Escobar would undoubtedly have his assassins on the lookout to kill him, constantly.

And Escobar controlled Medellin. A large part of the policed force there was in his pocket and the danger of being handed over to Escobar was great.

No member of the 200 strong team of Search Bloc was a native of the Medellin region. This meant that no-one had local knowledge. Still, there could be no risk of being betrayed by even a single member of the team.

Within 15 days of the search Martinez lost 30 of his men to Escobar's killers.

The casualties became so great that the Colombian police considered aborting the operation.

But the killings only angered the remaining members of Search Bloc and galvanized their resolve. On their behalf Martinez insisted that the hunt continue.

Then during a weekend trip home Martinez was visited by a retired colonel. He told Martinez that Escobar had said he and his family would be killed if he did not pass on an offer of $6000 000 to end the hunt.

Martinez was disgusted and he refused.

Martinez was horrified that Escobar had the means of discovering where he and his family lived, but at the same time he knew that the fate of Colombia was in his own hands.

Martinez immediately informed his superior of the bribe. The two agreed that it was a sign that they were getting closer to Escobar.

Escobar had other worries besides Martinez and Search Bloc.

Individuals whose lives had been savaged by Escobar had begun to band together and their number was growing.

These individuals called themselves Los Pepes, a name which was derived from *Perseguidos por Pablo Escobar*, 'Persecuted by Pablo Escobar.'

Despite the name, not all of all of them were vigilantes. Many were members of rival cartels. It was believed to have funded by the

Cali Cartel, right-wing paramilitary organizations and even by the United States.

Los Pepes was as ruthless as the Medellin cartel. Every day they hunted Escobar supporters and associates and killed them.

They exposed the bloodied corpses for all to see and placed signs on them reading 'For working with the drug terrorist and baby-killer, Pablo Escobar. For Colombia. Los Pepes.'

The terror was effective. Anyone suspected of aiding Escobar was killed. To avoid this fate many surrendered to Los Pepes. Escobar's insidious network disintegrated beneath him.

The Medellin Cartel was effectively smashed, but the ultimate prize, Escobar himself, remained elusive.

The Colombian government decided to invite the United States to help them directly.

There was a secret intelligence unit in Bogota called Centra Spike. It specialized in finding people, and set themselves to finding Escobar.

By now Escobar was continually on the run. His friends and associates were being picked off one by one. There were few people he could trust, and even they could be killed or bought. Escobar no longer had the power, or money, to keep them.

He often slept in the forests of the Medellin mountains. He could not use a telephone or a radio for fear that he would be discovered. Instead he communicated by courier.

On the run Escobar put on 20 kilograms. He could not fit into his regular clothes and had to find others. He whiled away his hours eating, sleeping and hiring teenage prostitutes.

He worried about his children.

Escobar planned to move his family out of the country. However his wife, son and daughter were under the protection of the Colombian government.

Escobar knew that the apartment building where they were living under heavy guard.

He managed to speak a number of times to his son.

Other family members and friends also sought the protection of the government, for Los Pepes were gradually killing off anyone related to Escobar.

Los Pepes also knew where Escobar's family was being held. They could have killed them easily. At one point they fired a grenade from a rocket launcher at the apartment.

But they were toying with Escobar to flush him out. They hoped that he would try and rescue his family. The government too was using the children as bait to bring him out into the open.

The End

Escobar celebrated his birthday on December 1 1993. The following day he was alone in his hideout with his bodyguard Alvero de Jesus Agudelo. His courier Jaime Rua and his aunt Luz Mila, who cooked for him, had gone out after breakfast.

On that day he looked unkempt and disheveled, a shadow of the man who had once terrorized Colombia. His waist had grown, so he bought jeans that were too long in the legs. He wore the leg cuffs turned up.

He wore a blue polo top and wore flip-flops. He was uncharacteristically bearded.

At one o'clock, posing as a journalist, he phoned his wife and briefly spoke to his children.

Martinez had allowed the call to go through so as to be able to trace it. As Escobar talked Martinez was already in pursuit with his men.

Driving up and down the Medellin street Martinez peered intently into the windows of the dwellings.

And then he saw him.

Martinez had never seen Escobar in the flesh, but he instantly recognized him from his photographs, despite the long curly black hair and beard.

Escobar, cell phone in hand, stepped back from the window. He probably recognized Martinez since he had spent so much time and money fleeing from him.

Martinez knew he had to act fast. Undoubtedly Escobar was even now alerting his gunmen. For every moment he hesitated his own life and the lives of his men were in greater danger.

He radioed all the units of Search Bloc in the area and ordered them to converge on the house.

His men knocked down the door of Escobar's house with a heavy sledgehammer.

Then the shooting started. Marinez's men swiftly seized the first floor, which was empty. They could see that there was a taxi waiting at the rear of the house, presumably for Escobar.

Agudelo, separated from his boss, fled to the rooftop. It was covered in loose yellowish tiles and surrounded by three walls.

By now dozens of Martinez's men were in the street surrounding the house. Some were standing on the tops of cars. They shot Agudelo several times before the fatal shot that caused him to fall to the ground below.

Escobar then appeared on the roof. He kicked off his flip-flops and hugged the walls of the roof so as to avoid ground fire.

There was a Search Bloc gunman on a roof above but he could not get a clear shot.

This break in the fire urged Escobar to make a break for the next rooftop.

Immediately a storm of bullets ensued, tearing up the tiles.

A Search Bloc team had secured the second story of the house and were making tentative steps toward the roof. They thought the gunfire was from Escobar's gunmen and radioed for help.

However it soon became clear that the fire was from the men on the ground.

There was a prostrate body on the floor of the rooftop. The gunfire died down. A shooter from the second floor cried out 'It's Pablo! It's Pablo!'

Men approached the body. A Major Aguilar turned the body over. He recognized the bloody face and radioed Colonel Martinez.

'Viva Colombia!' he shouted for all to hear. 'We have just killed Pablo Escobar!'

Aftermath

Search Bloc's account of how Escobar died has been challenged by rival drug traffickers, intelligence documents and Escobar's family.

On December 5 1993, three days after his death, the New York Times reported that he had been killed returning fire with a 9 mm Magnum pistol.

Some members of *Los Pepes* claim that they were present and that they delivered the fatal shot.

Yet other members of *Los Pepes*, notably one of its founders, Fidel Castano, emphatically deny this.

Escobar's own son, who now calls himself Sebastian, claims that he died by his own hand.

According to Sebastian his father had always told him that if he was cornered he would kill himself.

This seems a bizarre thing for a loving father to tell his son, but then Escobar was an extraordinary person.

In any case it is difficult to imagine how young Pablo could have known that his father actually killed himself.

His body was exhumed at the family's request in 2006 and a bullet hole was found in the right side of the skull, evidence, so the family claimed that Escobar killed himself.

Others have pointed out there was no evidence of gunpowder in the hole, indicating that the bullet that made it could not have been fired at close range.

Even after being shot Escobar would not go quietly. After the chaos and bloodshed he caused one might imagine that his funeral was an austere and private affair, involving perhaps just a priest and a few family members.

Instead there were thousands of mourners, all chanting his name and crowding the coffin.

At one point the mob even grabbed Escobar's silver coffin from the pallbearers and took it themselves to the burial site.

Pablo's widow saw a journalist and screamed 'You killed him!' The crowd looked toward the journalist and made for her.

The journalist escaped but the chaos continued. The people tried to touch the coffin, crying 'You can feel it! Pablo is present!'

A band played a local ballad 'But I keep on being King.'

The chaos became so great that Pablo's own family could not attend the burial.

Escobar was buried in the family graveyard he had purchased in the town of Itagui, just south of Medellin.

It is a quiet and peaceful place and hardly seems a reward for the violent life he led.

Even today fresh flowers are laid on his grave.

Outside Escobar's Medellin Colombia rejoiced.

In Bogota the newspaper headlines proclaimed 'Immortal Joy' and 'Delirium.'

President Cesar Gaviria addressed the people of Colombia, saying that 'Escobar's death was a step toward the end of drug trafficking, and that 'it is possible to defeat evil.'

The killing of Escobar was largely symbolic. The Medellin Cartel was already finished before his death and it was unlikely that he could have revived his fortunes even if he had survived.

But Colombia sorely needed symbols. For decades it had been crippled by war, factionalism, armed thugs and the drug trade. Escobar's death symbolized hope and more than hope. His demise demonstrated the power of the people.

The Cali Cartel, founded by Gilberto and Miguel Rodriguez and Jose Santacruz, who broke from the Medellin Cartel in 1977, continued their operations after destroying their greatest rival.

Escobar has assumed legendary status but few know the names of these men.

Nor do they know that the Cali Cartel became more powerful than Medellin had ever been.

At one point the Cali Cartel was responsible for 90% of the cocaine supply not only in the United States but in the entire world.

The violence of the Cali Cartel was characterized by a horrific form of social values. Elements of society considered '*desechabales*' (discardables) were slaughtered and often left in public as a warning to others.

These 'discardables' included homosexuals, prostitutes, petty criminals, street children and the homeless.

Many bodies of these unfortunates were thrown into the Cauca.

One municipality, Marsella, was bankrupted by the effort to remove corpses from the river and conduct autopsies.

After the death of Escobar the Colombian government and the US could now focus their attention on breaking up the Cali Cartel.

By mid-1995 all the heads of the Cartel had been arrested.

After this the Colombian government successfully broke up other cartels.

Nevertheless drug lords retain influence in Colombia and elsewhere to this day, owing in no small part to the reliance of the many paramilitary political factions which rely on drug money to finance themselves.

In order to fix the drug problem the Colombian government needs to fix the political problems, which are complex.

In 2016 the Colombian government signed a peace accord with FARC and by the end of February 2017 all its members had disarmed.

This is certainly encouraging, though FARC represents just a portion of the many paramilitary organizations in Colombia competing for power.

As of the time of writing Colombia remains the greatest supplier of cocaine in the world.

Cesar Gavirio's term as President of Colombia ended on August 7 1994 when he was succeeded by Ernesto Samper Pizano, whose campaign was financed by the Cali Cartel.

Samper was accused of being soft on the cartels.

Gavirio went on to become the seventh Secretary-General of the Organization of American States.

Hugo Martinez continued with the Colombia police until 2003 when he was elected Governor of the Department of Santander.

He was accused of collaboration with the AUC, or United Self-Defense Forces of Columbia, a paramilitary organization formed in 1997.

He was charged and arrested in 2011.

After most of the witnesses to his involvement with the AUC withdrew their testimony the Prosecution had to rely on the statements of one Colonel Julio Cesar Prieto.

Cesar gave evidence that Martinez had gained political office with the help of the AUC.

Martinez was sentenced to 9 years but served only 4 and half months before being granted probation.

Escobar's son Juan Pablo is now known as Sebastian Marroquin.

After his father's death his mother took his sister and himself to Mozambique. They then visited Argentina and eventually became citizens there.

He has a wife and daughter and works as an architect.

He does not like to talk about his father though he did write a book entitled *Pablo Escobar: My Father.*

The book was published in 2014 . It contains memories of his father. They are told plainly without any attempt to diminish the cruelty and ruthlessness of man.

Marroquin recounts the story of how his father left women's lingerie in his brother Roberto's shower when Roberto's wife came to visit. These horrible pranks almost destroyed their marriage. It was only when the couple was about to break up that Pablo revealed what he had done.

At any time Escobar asked one of his minions, called *El Gordo* to bring him a cup of coffee. Unbeknown to El Gordo Escobar popped Alka-Seltzers in his mouth which caused it to foam when he drank the coffee.

Escobar then accused El Gordo of poisoning him and made him beg for mercy at the point of a machine gun.

According to *Pablo Escobar: My Father* the war between the Medellin and Carli Cartels was started by one of the Cali leaders, Gilberto Rodriguez, refusing to send one of his men to Escobar.

This man had had sex with the former girlfriend of one of Escobar's friends, Jorge Pabon.

Pabon wanted revenge, and Escobar told Rodriguez 'whoever is not with me is against me'.

A few months later the Cali Cartel set off a car bomb in a building where Pablo's children were sleeping.

It is also in this book that Marroquin states that Escobar took his own life.

In 2009 Marroquin made a documentary with Argentinian-born director Nicolas Entel.

Marroquin was very reluctant to make a documentary about his father's life and had refused the approaches of several directors.

However he agreed on the condition that his sister was not shown in the film and that his father's name was not used in the title.

The theme of the film is reconciliation. In the documentary Marroquin visits the son of Luis Carlos Galan to ask forgiveness for his father assassinating Galan.

He also visits the son of Rodrigo Lara, the Colombian Minister of Justice murdered by Escobar.

Marroquin and his mother (then going by the name Victoria Hanaeo Vellejos) were arrested in Argentina on November 17 1999 on suspicion of money-laundering.

No charges were laid however.

The assumption that the Escobar family is still living off criminal proceeds will be hard to shake off.

Marroquin and his family have lived in fear of revenge attacks and kidnapping. At one point a distraught Marroquin even asked the Vatican for its protection.

Escobar today

Pablo Escobar is still very much alive in Colombia today.

In Medellin he is often referred to affectionately as *Pablito*, 'Little Pablo.'

Admirers still place flowers on his grave.

Escobar's face can be seen on t-shirts, coasters, place-mats, badges, posters and walls.

Many can point to their homes which Escobar built and where they live rent-free.

They can show you the schools and the churches he built for the poor, and they tell stories of the people who profited by their largesse.

Whatever they think of his other deeds, they see a man who helped people.

In a country like Colombia where poverty and misery are entrenched in society is irrelevant to his memory that all these things were bought with blood and cocaine.

Even the Catholic Church turned a blind eye to where the largesse that profits their parishioners came from.

One resident of Barrio Pablo Escobar, a neighborhood of Medellin built for the poor by Escobar explained his feelings toward Escobar.

'We respect the pain of his victims,' he said, 'but we ask people to understand our joy and gratitude, what it means to move out from a garbage dump to a decent house.'

Another Medellin resident, selling T-shirts with Escobar's image on them, explained 'People really like them because it's like wearing a [picture] of a Saint you have faith in.'

For others Pablo Escobar was nothing but a murderer and a tyrant who leaves a legacy of evil.

Among them is the son of murdered Minister of Justice Rodrigo Lara.

Commenting on his commercial presence, he says 'In a way it is an example of the triumph of culture embodied by Pablo Escobar, in which profit, making three bucks, is more important than anything else.'

The point is perfectly valid, but, as a state minister's son, he might never have felt the sting of poverty and so not quite understand the attitude of many of the Medellin poor.

Frederica Arellano, son of a man killed on the flight that was supposed to kill presidential candidate Cesar Gavrillia, agrees with Lara, and has an answer to the objection of the poor.

'Personally, coming back home and seeing his [Escobar's] face on the TV screen is an insult, a slap in the face,' he said.

'It is also sending quite a damaging message. It is saying: 'Go and become a criminal, because that way you can make money fast and lift your family out of poverty'.

In 2015 Netflix aired a crime drama series based on the life and deeds of Pablo Escobar.

The show, which continued for a second season in 2016, revived interest in the nefarious drug lord.

Some, including Sebastian Marroquin, have accused the show of romanticizing his father.

Judging from the variety of T-shirts bearing his image (one design has his head on a traditional image of the Sacred Heart of Jesus, hand raised in benediction) and other memorabilia, that accusation might be true.

The truth is that human beings are both horrified and fascinated by the depths to which human nature can sink.

Perhaps for most people, like myself writing this book and you reading it is no more than that.

Yet in countries like Colombia, where poverty and violence have forever gone hand in hand, the temptation to use violence as a tool is perhaps not only strong, but no temptation at all, because violence is seen as a condition of life.

Perhaps this is the most terrifying legacy Pablo Escobar left to Colombia: he bathed the country in so much blood that it knows nothing else.

There are in Colombia brave men and women still striving to show there is a better way.

Voices

In this last chapter we look at some of the sayings of Escobar. Reading them may offer some insight into the man's mind. They may suggest what motivated this evil mastermind.

Afterwards we shall see what others thought of him.

First, from the mouth of the man himself:

Everyone has a price, the important thing is to find out what it is.

Life is full of surprises, some good, some not so good.

Only those who went hungry with me and stood by me when I went through a bad time at some point in life will eat at my table.

Sometimes I feel like God…when I order someone killed – they die the same day.

There are two hundred million idiots, manipulated by a million intelligent men.

There can only be one king.

I prefer to be in the grave in Colombia than in a jail cell in the United States.

All empires are created of blood and fire.

I can replace things, but I could never replace my wife and kids.

I'm a decent man who exports flowers.

I have always considered myself a happy man. I've always been happy, I've always been optimistic, I've always had faith in life because I think the most difficult times always bring something. It brings experience, and it's the greatest thing to have in life.

here are two hundred million idiots, manipulated by a million intelligent men.

I'm sometimes accused of drug trafficking. It's an activity that for the time being, historically, shall we say has been declared illegal. It's illegal at the moment, but in the long run and in the future, we're going to show that it will head toward legalization.

Dirty money is in all economic sectors of the country.

The problem is not a matter of money. The problem is a matter of dignity.

Nothing gives a fearful man more courage than another's fear.

In modern business it is not the crook who is to be feared most, it is the honest man who doesn't know what he is doing.

Now some quotes from others about Pablo Escobar. These are the opinions not of his powerful friends and enemies, but of ordinary Colombians, all old enough to have memories of Escobar.

'Escobar was known as The Robin Hood of the poor. He built and gave away houses for many people. He built parks for kids with scarce resources, football fields, gave away money and sponsored many people who needed help. Those are enough reasons for those who venerate and admire him. Yes, it is true that he did much more than the government did for some cities but that does not justify the bad he did with his way of taking control over the business of drug trafficking. So what happens to a person in their search for control and power that wants to take the whole world on? In reality his good deeds end up being only strategies to camouflage a form of crime. More importantly, the legacy or teachings he left the next generations was bad. They want to live a luxurious life and obtain it the easy way. I refer to those who want to become rich selling drugs, kidnapping, stealing, killing and extorting people. They don't want to study and obtain things through hard work. Those are the reasons that for me Pablo was one of the worst Colombians in our history.'

-Kelly, 30,

'He did a lot of good things. He created houses for the poor and gave houses to many mothers who've never had one. He gave jobs and helped people who needed it. He wanted to change the country and most importantly the government. That's why he got into politics. When he did, he aspired to be a president to change many things to change the country. But, the government went against him and took him out of the running. So he sought vengeance and killed many people. He placed bombs and even exploded a plane. He implemented a lot of violence and many innocent people died. But, I liked him because he was going to take Colombia out of poverty and make it a rich country. The government runs Colombia wrong. Colombia is rich in everything, but the politicians steal the resources. So he got into politics and the Minister of Justice, Rodrigo Lara, complained saying that he had been in jail and was a narco-trafficker. They kicked him out like a dog. That's where he started the war towards its leaders.'

Ruben, 41.

'He is a man who ruined the reputation of a country. Due to him and his people we are known all over the world as a country of drugs and they stereotype us as narco-traffickers. When I lived in Medellin, I lived in fear and terror. I remember each night they would put a new bomb in a different part of the city. He then moved on to other cities like Bogota and Cali. That time marks me because we could not leave the house at night and the number one program to watch in TV was the news. For me the saddest aspect of all was the prostitution and hit men because it is still something common in my country.'

-Natalia, 45.

'He had so much influence in Colombia that he changed a generation. Those people saw how easy drug trafficking was so they didn't go to college or work because it was easier for them to make money selling drugs. When that ended, all those people didn't know how to do anything and they were already in their 30s or 40s. So what happened was that they started becoming hit men or extortionists. Just being delinquents because they didn't know how to do anything. Many people I knew ended up like that. At one point they had money, houses, women, cars and then all of a sudden nothing, begging people for money for a soda.'

Javier, 42.

'Aside from the horrible and terrorizing he did, I liked his personality. He was a person who whatever he thought, made reality. And he had big ideas. He helped do the impossible possible for people. He immortalized himself because of what he did. Despite the years that have passed the people still know who he is and remember the great things he did. Like reconstruct the entire barrio for people of low resources. He had his zoo with some of the most exotic animals in the world and had a huge car collection. Like I said, I like him because what he wanted, he made possible. Nothing was impossible for him'

-Alejandro, 34.

'I think it's impossible to love a man that did so many damage to a country. He's the main man who brought drugs to Colombia. He's the biggest assassin of all. He killed kids, elderly, and teenagers with no signs of remorse. He was dedicated to killing the police, he paid millions to get them killed. He left many children orphans, women and men widows, because he killed with no compassion. For me it's as if he did not exist because he did bad things to our country, our society and his own family.'

-Rubiela, 64.

'At first he was an admirable man who helped many people. He wanted to be Robin Hood. He stole from the rich to give to the poor. When he started wanting power is when he turned into fiend and terrorized the country. It's hard to say if he's a hero or a villain. At first he was a hero and at the end a villain. He put the country at its knee.'

-Daniel, 34.